# 30 Sloths to Color
# DIY BOOKMARKS

Happy Sloth
Coloring Bookmarks

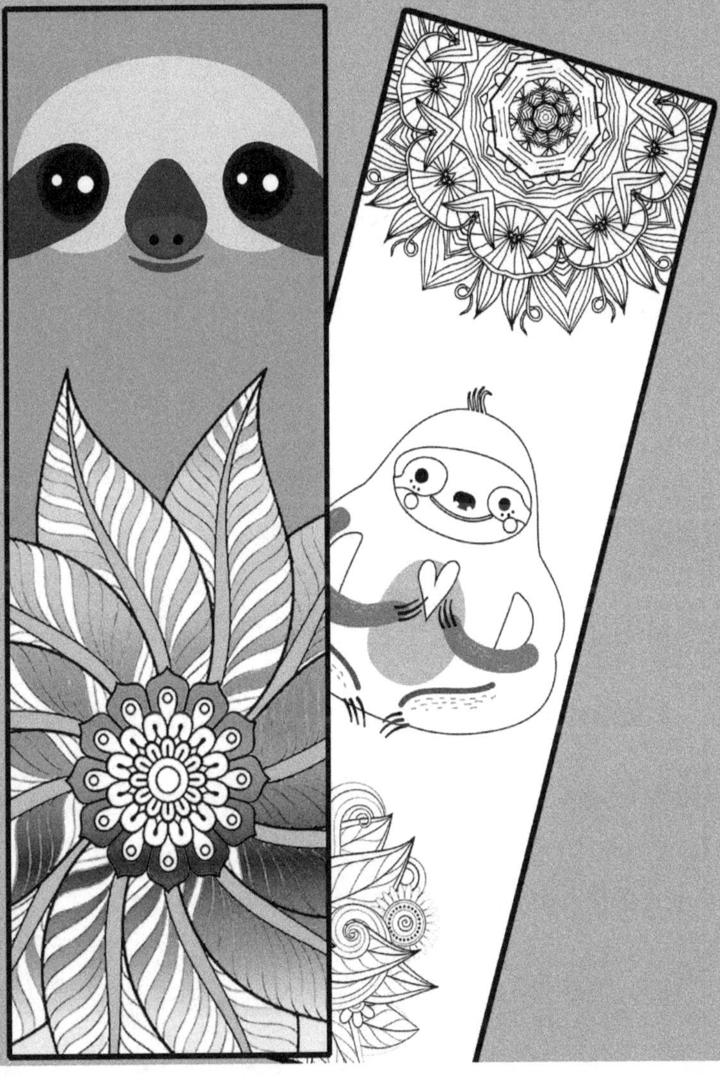

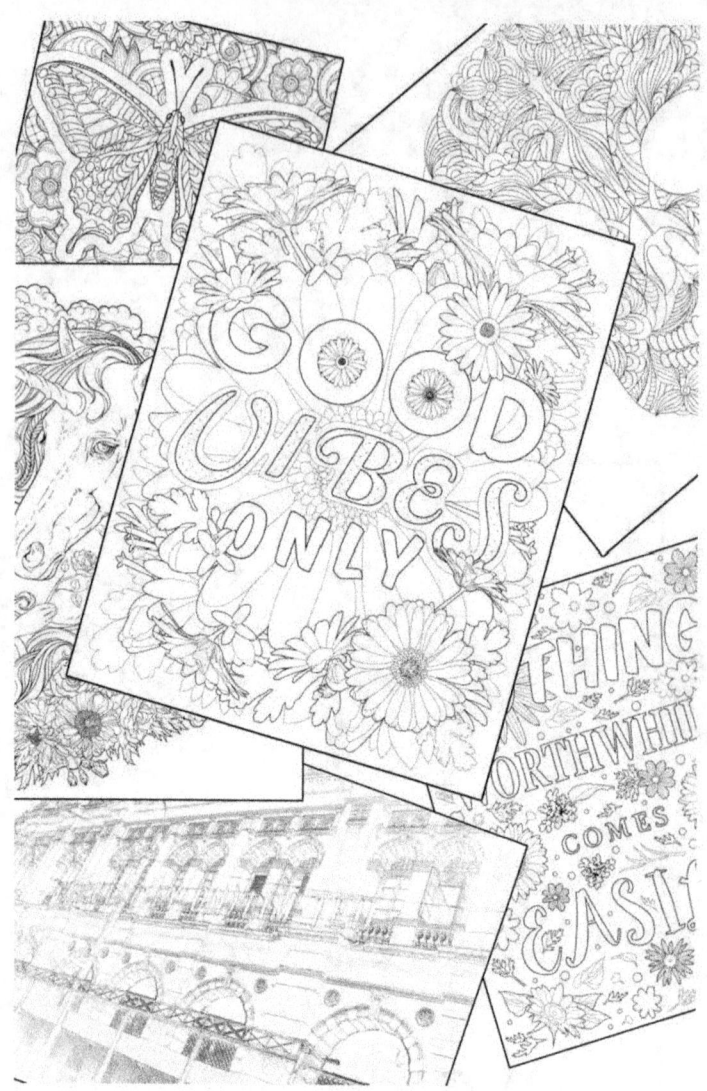

**Join Us >> bit.ly/get_sample_free**

- Get Free "Reviw Copies" of our New releases
- Exclusive offers and book giveaways
- More events from our community

**Thank you**

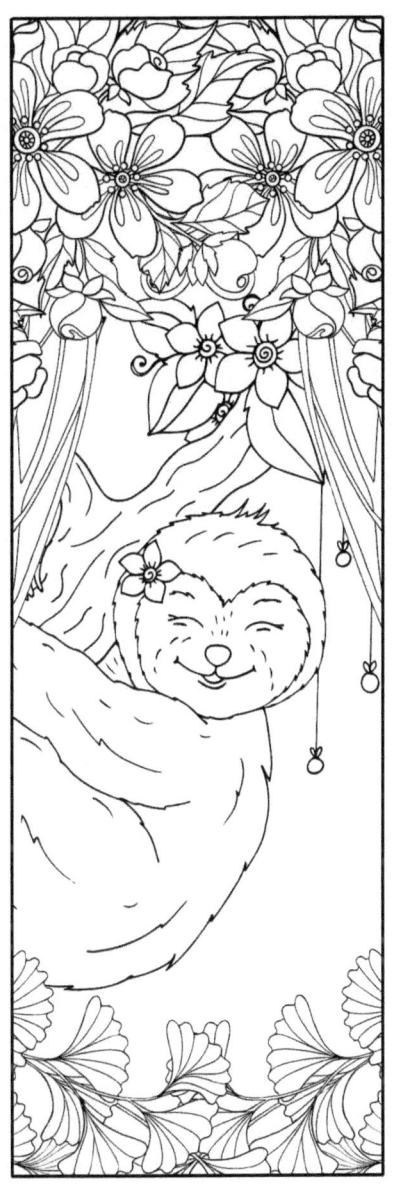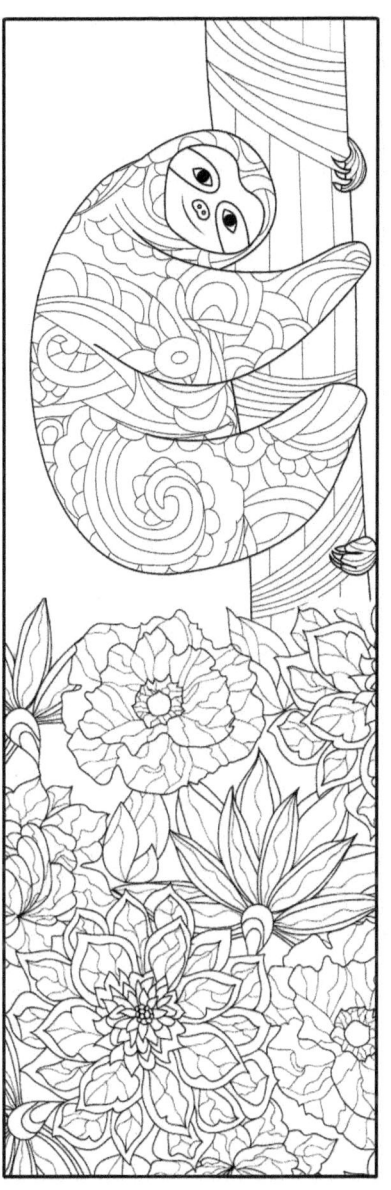

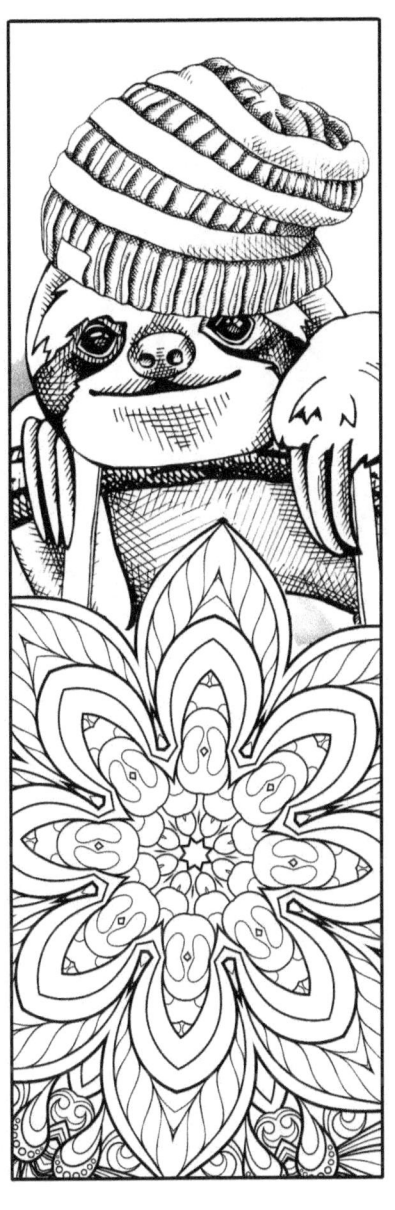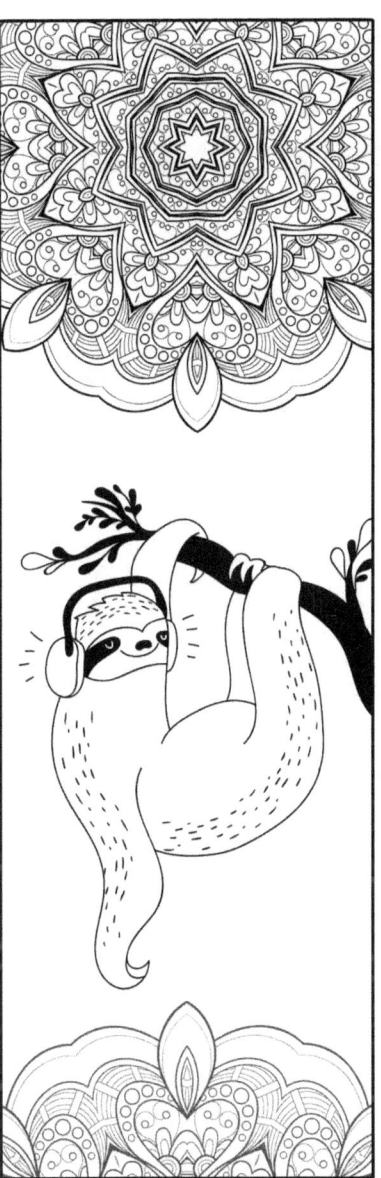

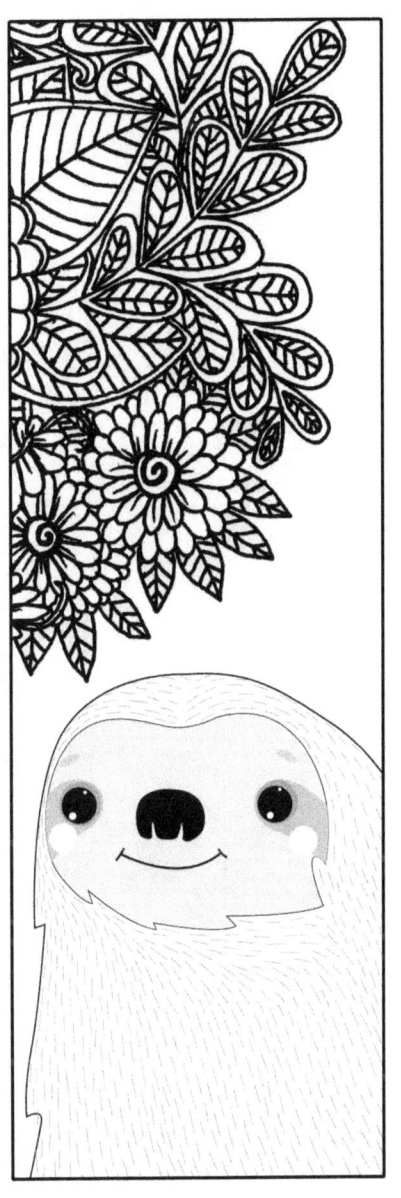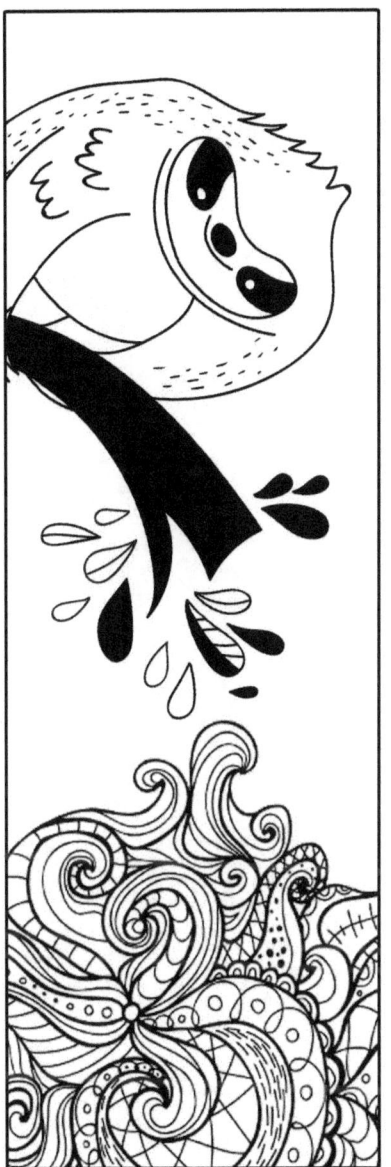

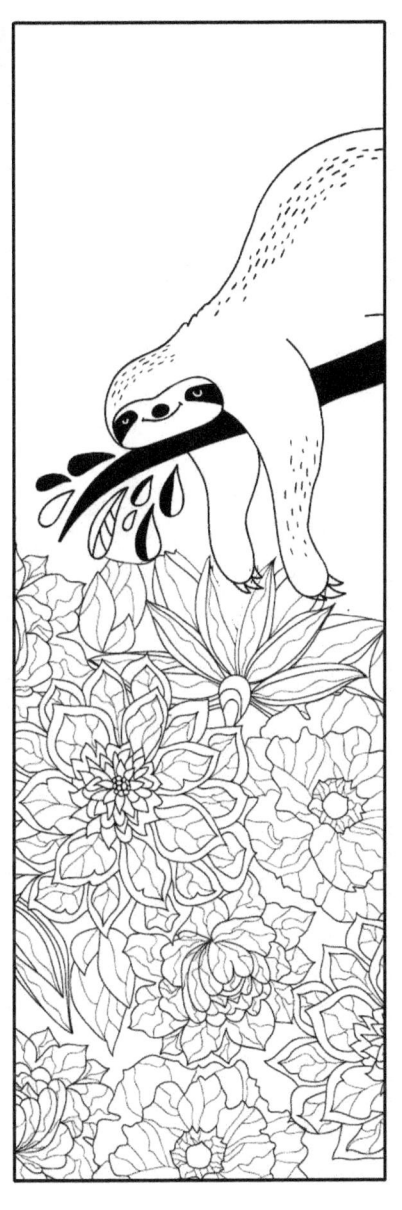
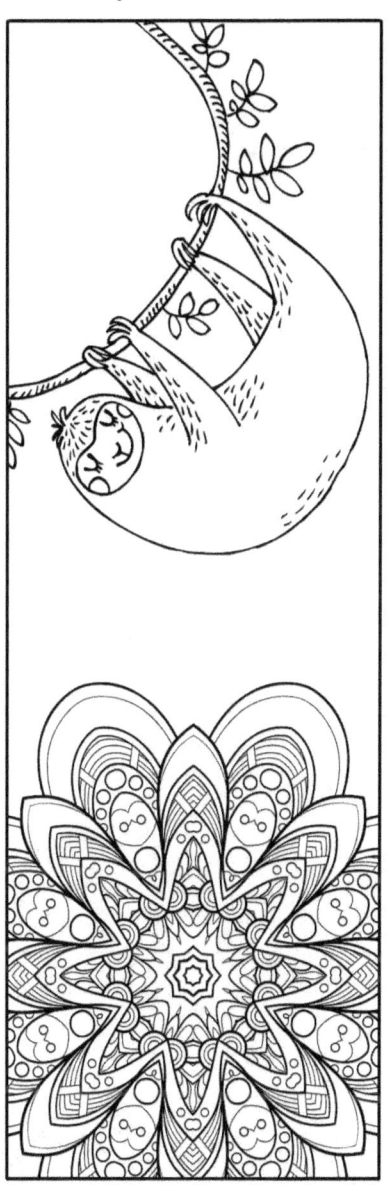

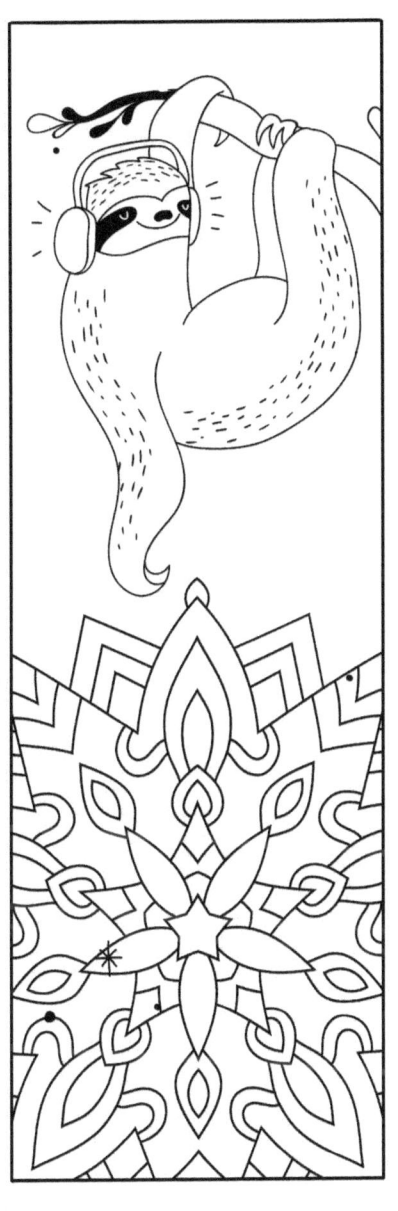

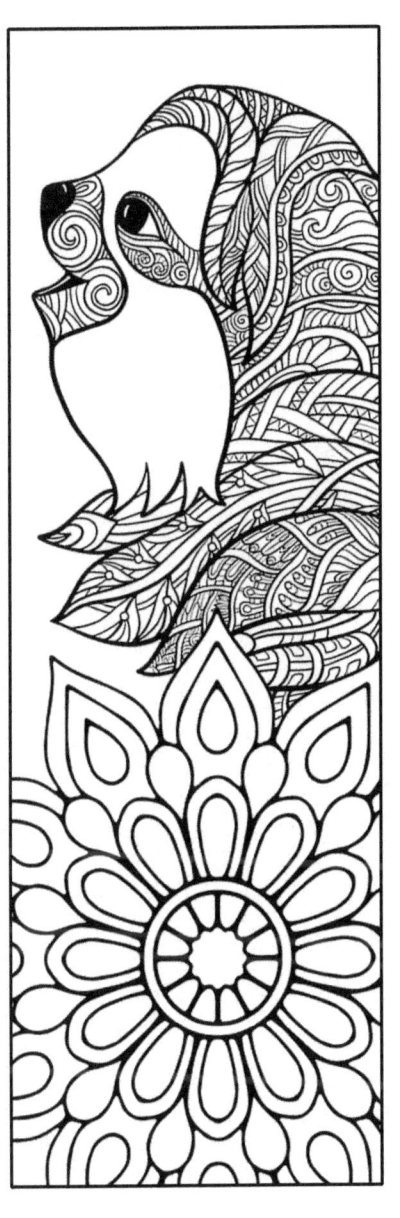
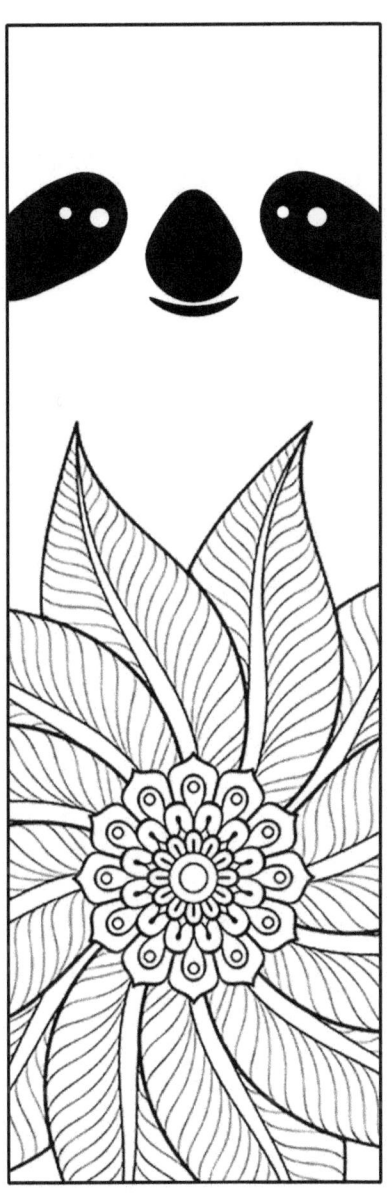

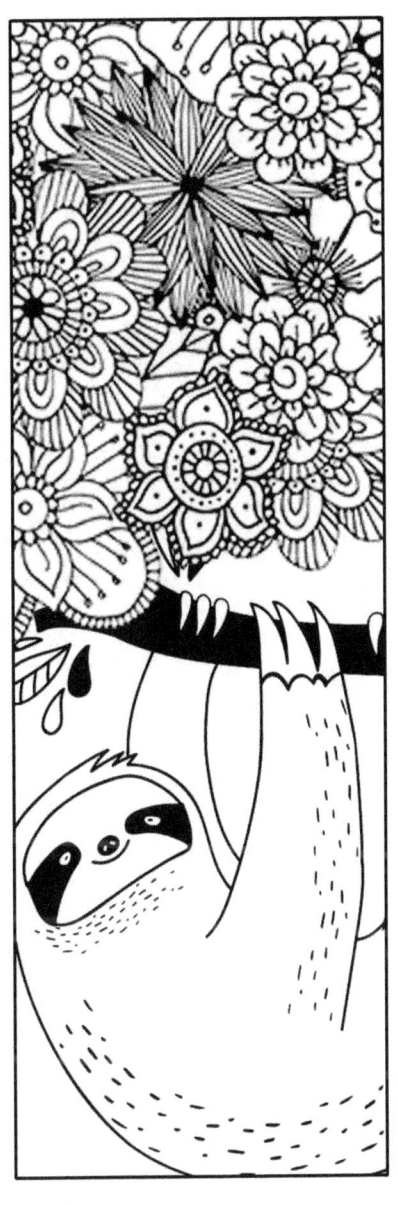
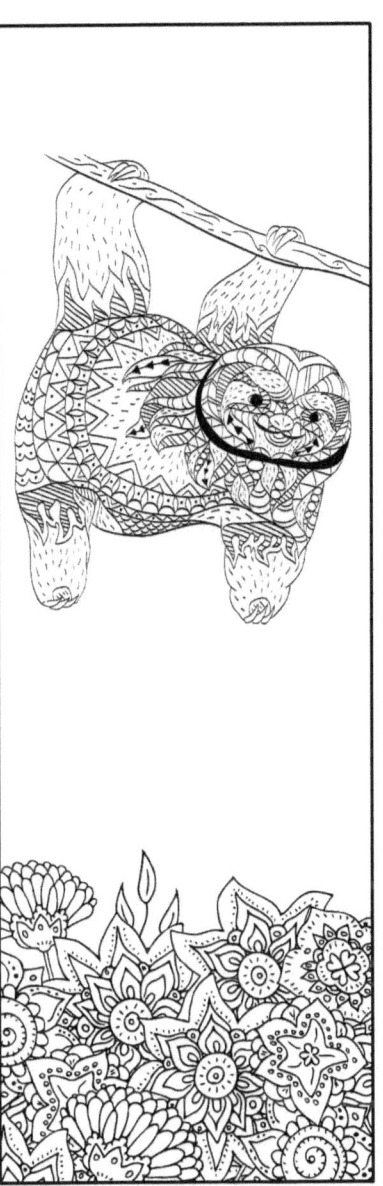

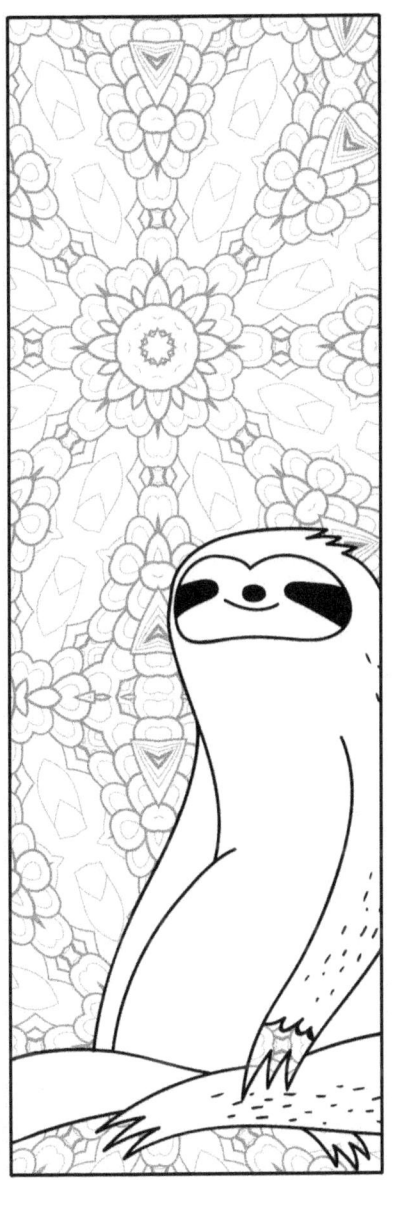
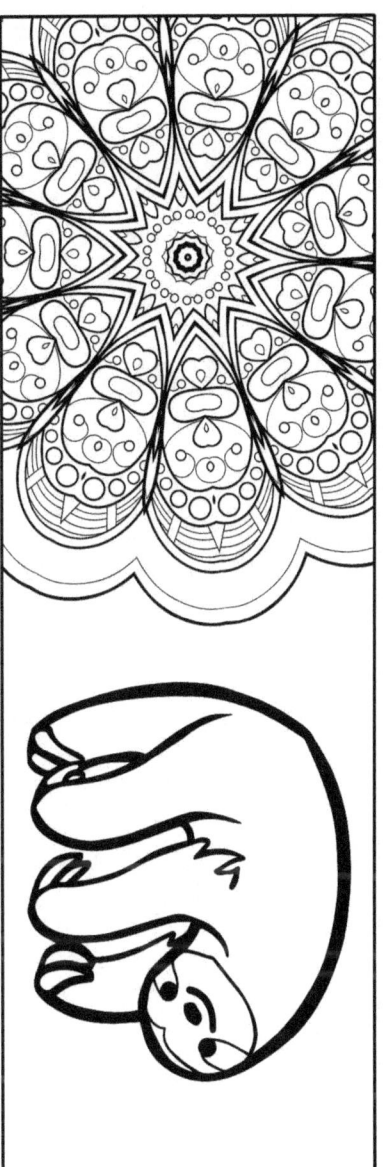

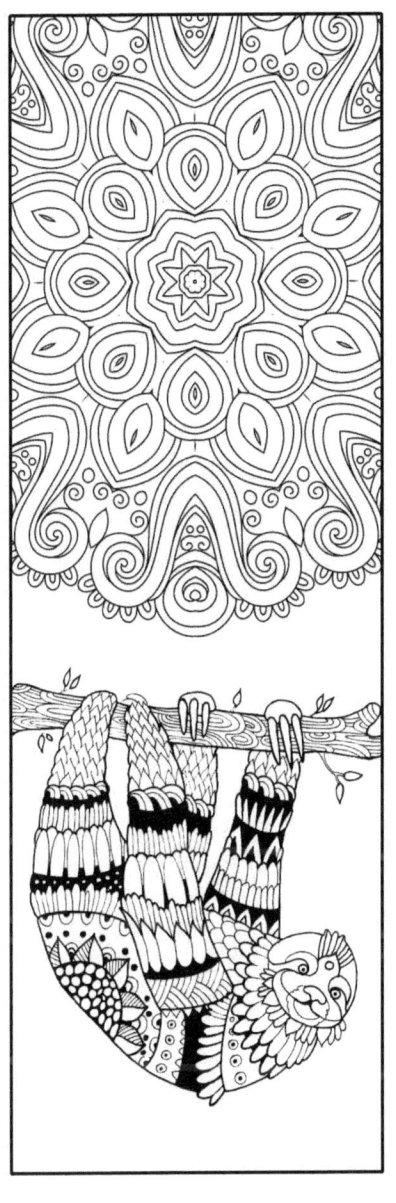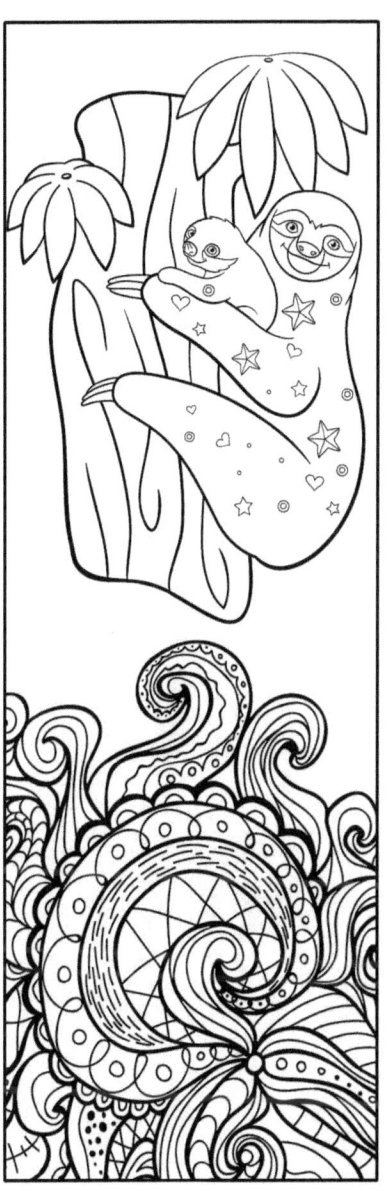

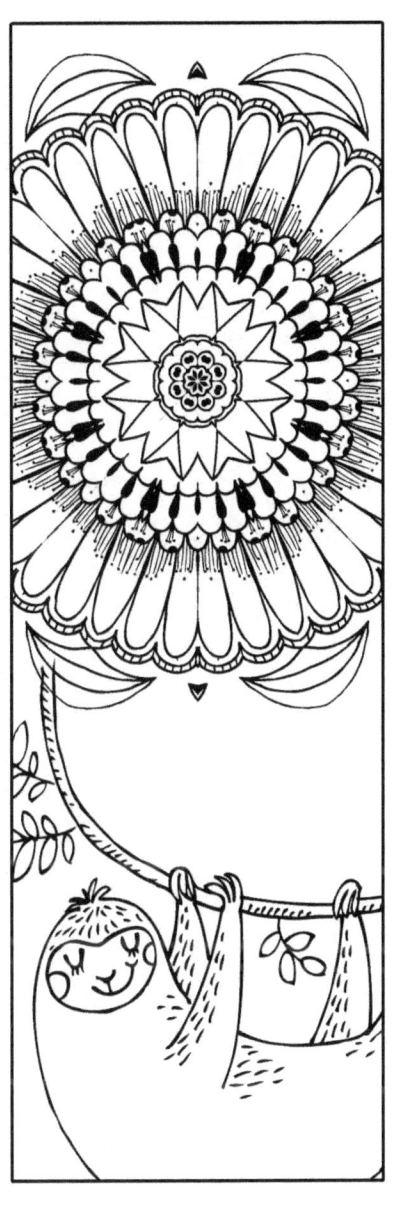
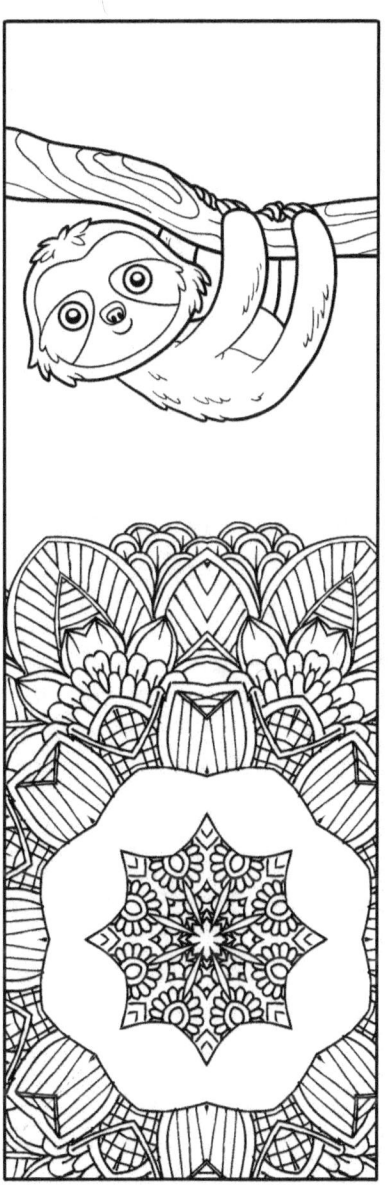

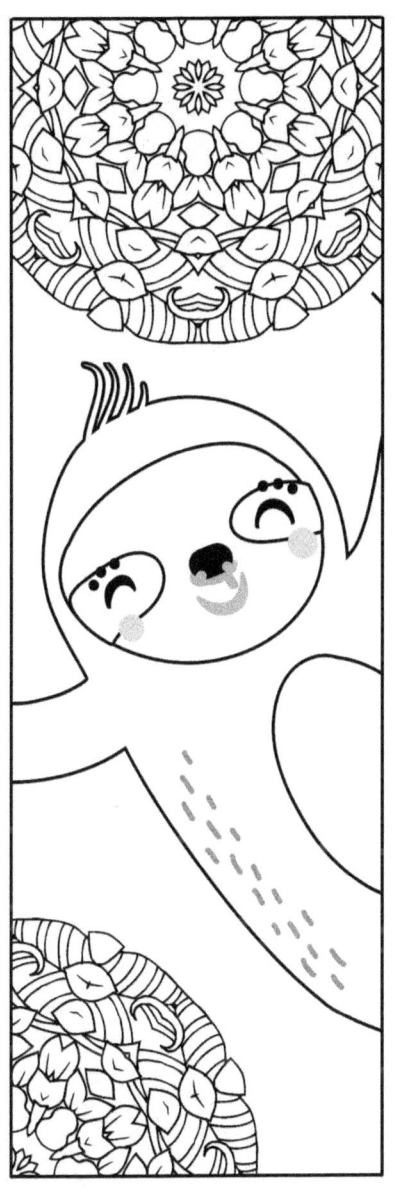
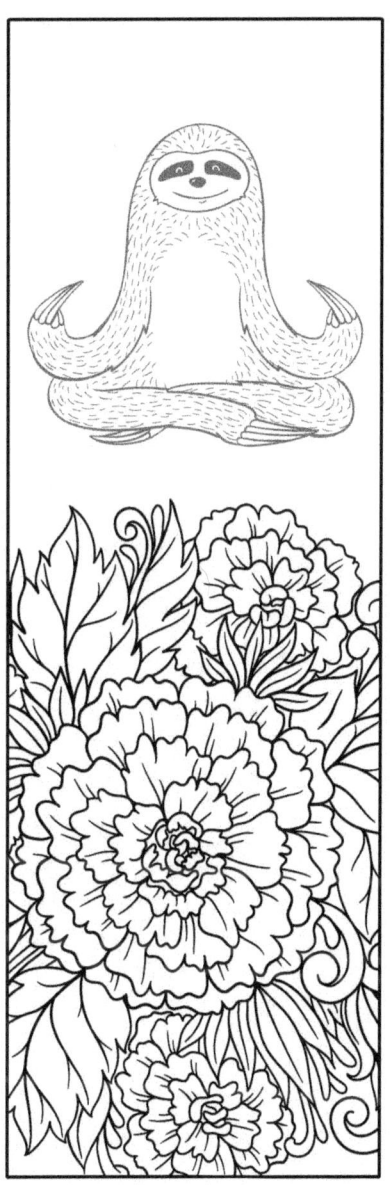

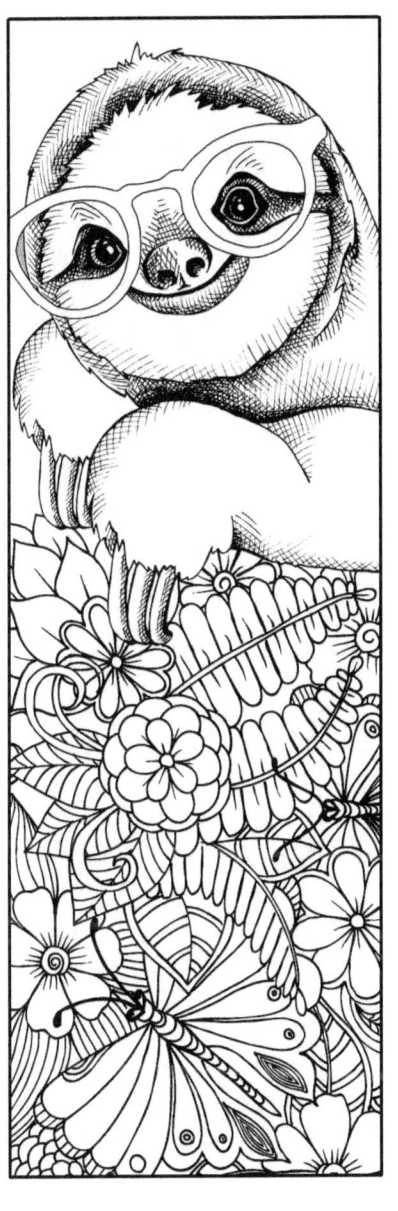
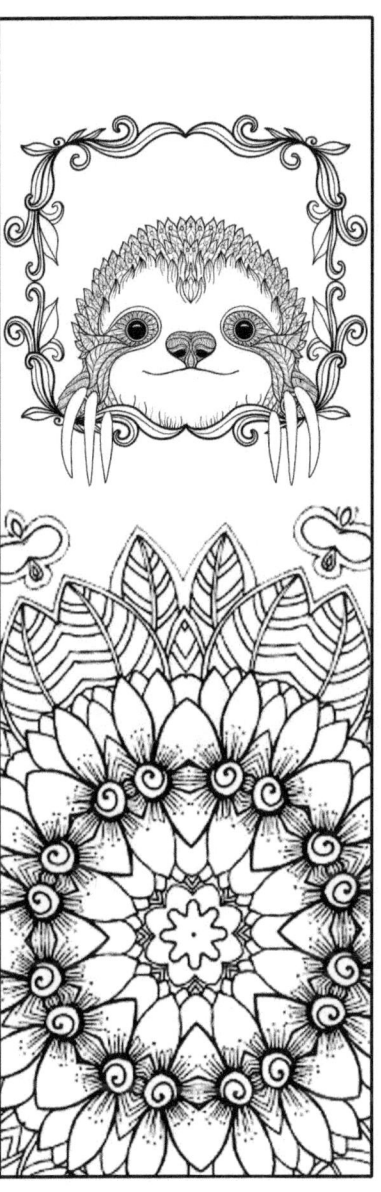

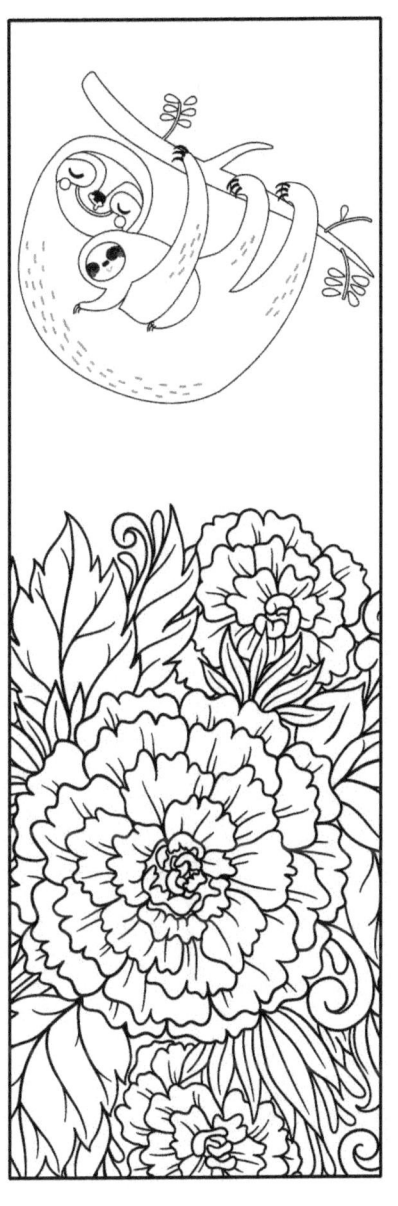
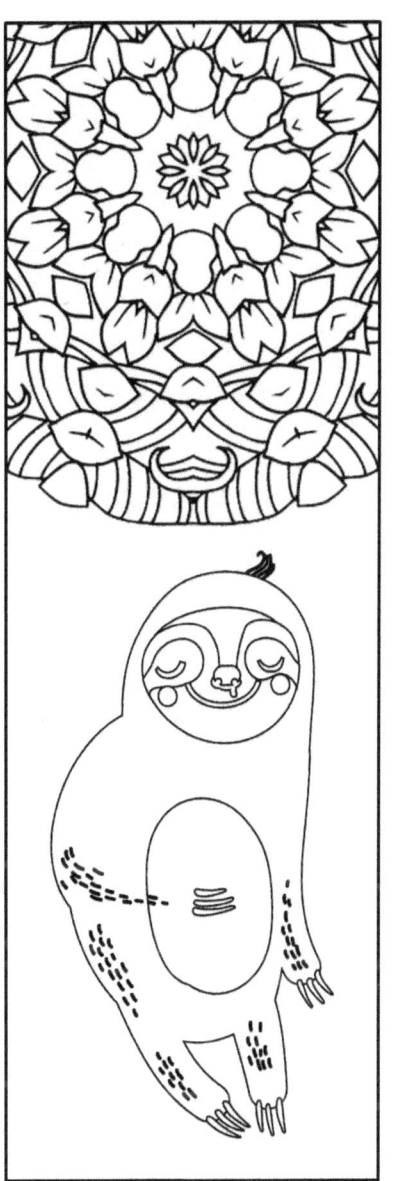

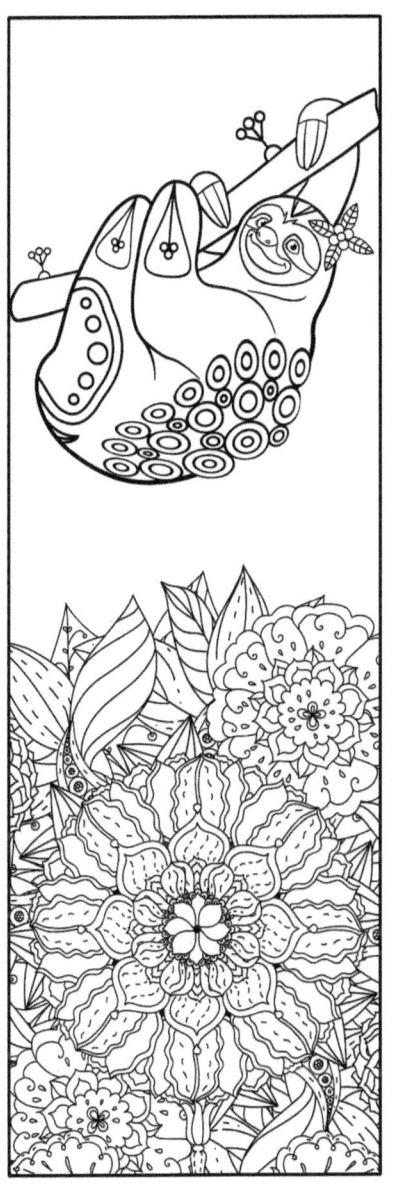
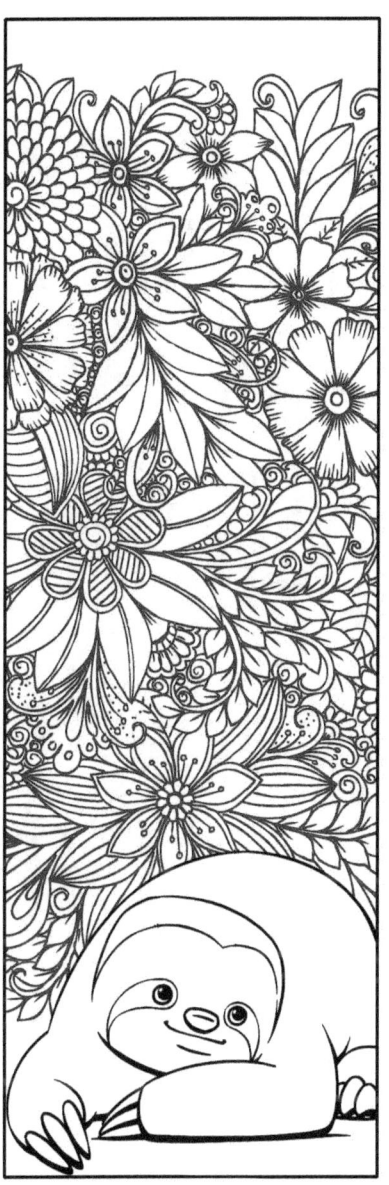

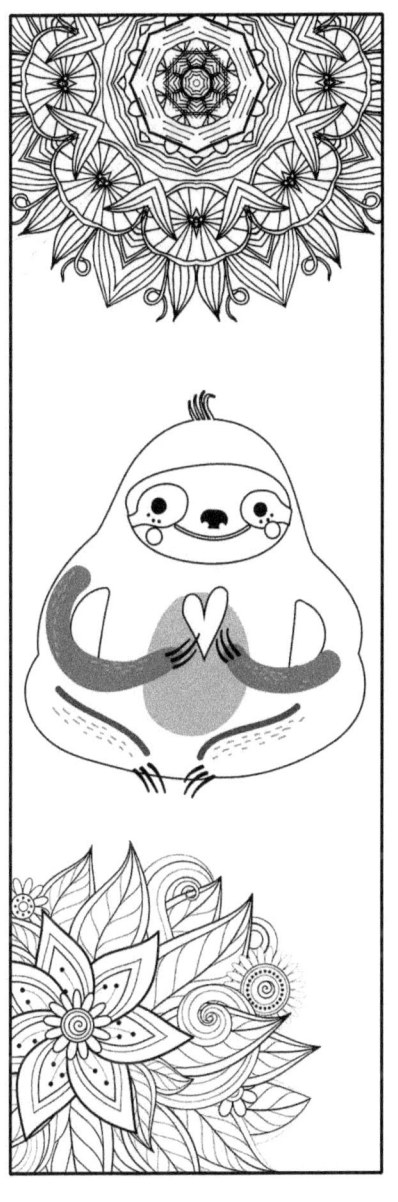
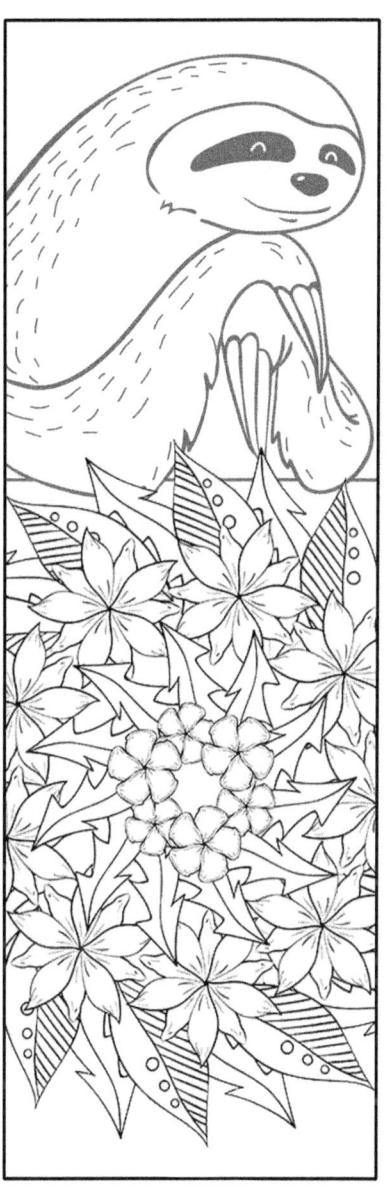

www.ingramcontent.com/pod-product-compliance
Lightning Source LLC
Chambersburg PA
CBHW050254230526
45470CB00005B/2256